exo—*prefix*. Outside; external; exoskeleton [Gk. exo, outside of < ex, out of.]

geo.des.ic . . . 2. Geodetic. —*n. Math.* In three-dimensional Euclidean space, a curve whose principal normal at any point is the normal to the surface on which the curve occurs: the shortest line between two points on any mathematically derived surface.

The American Heritage Dictionary

For my father, L. R. Dollens

This is my favorite picture of my dad. It was taken in the mid-1940s in Waco, Texas. My dad, on the left, is working on a model with my Uncle Dean. Early on my father taught me model building in our Southern California garage and that is where warped surfaces, stressed skins, airfoils, struts, braces, and the smell of model dope entered my thoughts (and blood stream).

Cover:
Tumbleweed, YuccaTruss model,
and 3D StudioMAX models of UmbrellaTruss II.

Back Cover:
Tumbleweed, plant section, cells, and TowerTruss.

Lumen, Inc.
3900 Paseo del Sol
Santa Fe, New Mexico 87505
www.sitesarch.org

t e u x m i b t l i e n w g e e e x dordium

*EX*ODE

See! them
arising anew:

Exiting exodus ex officio: *amaranthus*, tumbling tumbleweed tumbled
trussed and thrust (and counter thrust) and weeded, seeded, barbered but barbed
untumbling tumbleweed tumbling up, their terra pledge new plighted—*don't*
you listen.
Bid *amaranthus*, the exordium EXODESIC and GEODESIC ±, the ode
geodesic,
a geode weede, a geonosy posy, *amaranthus all his beauty shed*, all skeletal
not withered: $\alpha + \mu\alpha\rho\alpha\iota\nu\epsilon\iota\nu$
this thistle Russian thrust and trussed (and counter thrust)—exotic exodic of
branch and barb (barbered, but not unbarbed) into treed trussed-truss thrust
(and counter thrust)
of trust and bond bound (yes, bound) in and like this:

TUMBLE

R

tUmble

S

S

& T

R

TUMBLE

S

t

truSs

m

b

l

e

but *don't you listen to him*. "Fame is no plant that grows on mortal soil," keep amovin, man, it tumbles like the tumblin tumble weed *and spreads the burning sand* till trussed into a thrust (and counter thrust) of exordium exotic from the Siberian Wilde to the Faith Sainted, introited upon a vaulting voluted with voluper papered—aloft in a tryst of thrust (and counter thrust) trussed, foiled. Treed. Flown not flying, tumbled not tumbling, thrust and thrusting (and counter thrusting). New branched ored ode, foil flown. Flight stayed.

> Stemming: sprig, shoot, sprout—still
> branch, bud, bloom—stretch
> a skin balloon, curved, down—strut struts

See them arising renewed anew, reappearing in ritual digital, the piering peered pirouette digital—tented trees

All ex/o/de, exodesic. *With water!* Without. An ectoplantsmic exo for your inner tryst: with/out—inner and under the upper over and outer

Ronald Christ

Skewered Clouds
Duncan Brown

I currently have this fixation that the future of architecture relies on small firms creating interventions in the existing built fabric. Interventions that are not necessarily complete buildings or complexes but preciously crafted commentaries. Nothing is really new, only recycled, reworked.

However questionable parallels between architecture and literature are, the activities of the French group Oulipo, the Workshop for Potential Literature, springs to mind as a model, and this is how I view the work in *Exodesic*. While the Oulipo's formal interests in literary structure suggest an association with the abstract tenets of Beaux Arts or High Modernism, in architecture interpretation is also possible in material terms.

Architecture is a formal elaboration of spatial types through different, often circumstantial and contextual means. The single-volume space, whether it is a stone dwelling or a large steel hangar, to the multicelled warren, whether it is an adobe pueblo or a concrete Ministry of Information. As technology advances new means and methods, the opportunity for interpreting these types increases.

The tumbleweed of old used to symbolize the restlessness of Hollywood's Western heroes. It is really not much more than a common weed, growing to a certain age before being blown free from its roots. Introducing the tumbleweed to architecture and exploring its material qualities and digital extension act as variants of a critical regionalism—eco-structures for the Nineties.

Exodesic had a long gestation period. Twenty years of being an architectural critic and editor before Dollens made what must be seen as a cathartic move from Manhattan to Santa Fe. Many of the texts and articles from this earlier period serve as the background to ideas behind the TumbleTruss series.

Indeed, Dollens has said in a recent e-mail that an article on Louis Sullivan in SITES 1 spurred his interest in cell development for design inspiration.[1] Truss names are contained in his essay on Bolles-Wilson's "Ninja Architecture," describing an alternative attitude to electronic consumer society.[2] The article on the "Structures of Nomadics: Umbrellas, Huts, and a Tower" in *Reports 4* addresses the contemporary relevance of the buildings and organization of nomad life.[3]

Multiple ways of making—assembling, skinning, and casting—are coupled with a progression of types—columns, canopies, tents, and larger complexes. Each of the models is iconic, identifiable in a graphic way. The process is kept loose and open to accident. Advances are made at each stage, and exchange occurs between the real and the digital. The project both evolves and *e*-volves electronically.

The first scanned pieces of tumbleweed (p. 16) were suggestive of wildly organic trusses. They had the silhouette of gothic tracery, but lost the twisted depth of the original. Repeated in series, they could have been the enclosure for a large stadium.

The UmbrellaTruss (pp. 18-19) was the first digital evolution of the project. A truss outline was spun about its axis to create a large canopy. Images of the second iteration (pp. 20-21) really give you an idea of what it might be like to inhabit a TumbleTruss—the angular walls of a stealth cathedral. Skinning the frames further articulates the complexity of enclosure outlined by the thin, twisted truss members.

Subsequent models develop a palette, as different types of handmade paper and fabric are applied to the tumbleweed. This is not, however, a craft exploration, but more akin to Naum Gabo's investigation of different materials—an organic constructivism. Fiberglass has been studied, and more recently concrete and Amazon latex.

Further development increases the number of truss components in an assembly and the surface area being skinned with paper. More recently, the planes of the FoilTruss (p. 72) suggest floor plates grouped around an atrium and return to the use of the tumbleweed's original overall form. There is a greater suggestion of enclosure and, consequently, occupation.

Like nomad tents, the TumbleTrusses are not so much site-specific as capable of being located anywhere. To date, the TumbleHouse (p. 25) is the only project where a program has been indicated. The canopy form suggests primitive shelter and by association extends utility to the other models. As physical and digital conceptual models, the trusses are scaleless and open to interpretation. This parallels an e-mail comment of Dollens, in reference to the form of a candelabra, that "to Jujol everything was architecture and that scale determined its function."

The Plan B installation (pp. 53-61) is a captured encampment of skewered clouds. Cantilevered arms of a drifting space colony. The installation presents a nomad urbanism. Models, independently dynamic, collectively charging the air between them. Space is being cultivated, cultured.

Another interpretation might be: the tumbleweed, a parasitic nomad, has been used, almost like a postcard, to re-imagine the architecture of another place and culture, in this case Barcelona. Where over a period of twenty years Dollens spent a considerable amount of time.

It was not until I went to Barcelona that the TumbleTruss project really struck home. The angular lines of Miralles's Icaria Passage, multiple trusses rooted in the ground, activating the space between apartment blocks. Gehry's fish on the ocean promenade, the copper-skinned framework of steel. The twisted volumes of the iron railings at the Gaudí Museum in Park Güell.

Most significant of all is Jujol, who has been the subject of extensive study by Dollens since 1981.[4] The garden pergola at Can Negre (p. 17) has an uncanny resemblance to a TumbleTruss. The scratchy angular qualities

Church at Vistabella. Vistabella, Spain. 1918-1923. Josep Maria Jujol.

of weed fragments are like Jujol *sgraffiti*. The intersecting masonry vaults of the Church at Vistabella are undoubtedly related to the New Mexican TumbleTrusses.

In "Jujol reSurfaced" Dollens writes how Gehry's Guggenheim Museum has helped alter his appreciation of Jujol. He quotes Borges: "In the critic's vocabulary, the word *precursor* is indispensable, but it should be cleansed of all connotations of polemics or rivalry. The fact is that every writer creates his own precursors. His work modifies our conception of the past as it will modify the future." [5] Appropriately, *Exodesic* helps animate Jujol for me.

Imagine you had the gene patent for tumbleweed and could completely determine how it grew. New structures nurtured by design. *Exodesic* represents the conceptual model for reverse engineering a future architecture. Future lists of construction types will include the cultivated. There will be buildings. The seeds have been formed.

1. Dennis L. Dollens. "The Bayard Building." SITES 1 (New York: Lumen, 1979).

2. _____ . "Toward Ninja Architecture/ HyperarchiTEXTure." *Offramp*. Southern California Institute of Architecture. Vol. 1. #4. 1991. Also see: "Ninja Architecture Seen from New York." *El Croquis*. Madrid. March 1991.

3. _____ . "Structures of Nomadics: Umbrellas, Huts, and a Tower." *Reports 4*. New York: Storefront for Art & Architecture. November 1992.

4. _____ . *Josep Maria Jujol: Five Major Buildings, 1913-1925*. (Santa Fe: SITES Books, 1994).

5. _____ et al. *Jujol's Universe*. (Barcelona: Col.legi d'Arquitectes de Catalunya, 1998).

Structural Truss + Tumbleweed =

TumbleTruss Project is a series of physical models and related electronic, 3D models and graphics that I developed as design experiments dealing with curving forms and warped surfaces. After moving to Santa Fe from New York in 1995, I sought to relate my architectural interests to botanic material and nonlinear research found in this region. First, I wanted to build models with branching, trusslike structures that are irregular and twisted—tumbleweeds as raw material fit this bill perfectly. Common to the entire West, despised by most people, these 19th-century emigrant weeds from Siberia proved ideal for my idea of generating a series of complex-curved structural components that might allow me to build skewed forms, contours, and parts.

In many ways the tumbleweed truss is a readymade in the Duchampian mode. The weed's overall globular form breaks down into curvilinear branching segments that create an inner, self-bracing structure; essentially, the branches are de facto trusses. Their curving forms with interlocking cross-bracing made them attractive to me as did the idea of transforming elements of a natural structural organization into an artificial one. (I was also very attracted to tumbleweeds for being pests and generally worthless.) And their natural, swaying curvature made the individually harvested and trimmed branches ideal as irregular wooden components, suited to both model building and desktop scanning. Nomadic by natural design, these rolling weeds not only traveled over our site, they also grew everywhere.

Initially I "built" the trusses on my scanner's glass flatbed, that is, laying out trimmed tumbleweed pieces in various truss forms, scanning them, and then adjusting them in Photoshop. From Photoshop I then exported the digital images to FreeHand, where I began graphically manipulating them. I was also building physical models at the same time. Early in this process I realized that a flatbed scanner was a liability: it illuminated a single elevation's curvature but could not account for side-to-side oscillation in three dimensions. This noted, I determined that the project would need to be drawn in a 3D modeling program to render curvature from all views and that the real models would need to move away from mimicking standard trusses.

From this point I began building more complex physical models that I could not scan. These models are made of selected and trimmed tumbleweed branches reassembled and glued into a TumbleTruss structure. Once a structural frame was complete, I "skinned" or sheathed it, at the start with Japanese rice papers or a loose-weave gauze overlaid with aluminum, copper, or gold leaf. Soon, though, I wanted a material from our site and began collaborating with a local papermaker to produce pulps specifically for the trusses and then to apply the wet sheets immediately onto the structural frames. Initially, we worked with flax and kenaf pulps, but I wanted a fuller material connection to the Santa Fe area and dug up narrow-leaf yucca plants from our yard for experimental pulpmaking. The yuccas produced an off-white, speckled paper that can be seen on many of the models.

Once models are complete (or sometimes concurrent with their building), I draw them in 3D StudioMAX, Extreme 3D, and occasionally in AutoCAD. The resulting digital models and drawings are not intended to precisely follow the physical models; rather, they are the first steps in manipulating the abstract forms resulting from the semirandom assembly of the tumbleweed curves and their resulting warped surfaces. In a sense, I think of the physical models as studies or form-seeds that are first sprouted, then grown electronically—seeds that could, eventually, be programmed as self-generating architecture and whose resulting virtual architecture could then be rebuilt physically in a repeating cycle of virtual and physical development.

What follows here is a mostly chronological view of the TumbleTruss Project—with a definitely qualified *mostly*. Often I find that something I began months or even years ago re-engages my attention, and I go back to extrude new elements or create new animations, etc. The text is equally adjusted; it is a running journal of sorts, with call-outs, quotations, and fragments of thoughts, many connected, but a few project- or even page-specific.

Tumbleweed: solarized section of immature plant with
400x insert of tumbleweed cells.
Opposite: detail, mature tumbleweed.

Tumbleweed, Russian thistle, Chenopodiaceae (Goosefoot family)
A rounded, bushy, much branched annual, 1/2 to 3 feet tall, reproducing by seed. Stems are usually red or purple striped. Leaves are alternate; the first are long, string-like and soft, with later leaves short, scale-like and tipped with a stiff spine. Inconspicuous green flowers are borne in axils of upper leaves, each flower accompanied by a pair of spiny bracts.
Seeds are spread as mature plants break off at ground level and are scattered by the wind as tumbleweeds. Rapid germination and seedling establishment occur after only brief and limited amounts of precipitation. Since Russian thistle was introduced (from Russia) in the late 1800s, it has become one of the most common and troublesome weeds in the drier regions of the U.S. It is well adapted to cultivated dryland agriculture, but is also found on disturbed wastelands, overgrazed rangeland, and even some irrigated cropland. Barbwire Russian thistle (S. paulsenii Litv.) is similar in overall appearance but is generally more coarse and robust, with broader and more rigid spine-tipped leaves. Also referred to as S. kali L., S. kali L. var. tenuifolia Tausch, S. kali L. var. ruthenica (Iljin) Soo, and S. pesitfer A. Nels.

Weeds of the West
Western Society of Weed Science

The skeleton begins as a continuum,
and a continuum it remains all life long.
The things that link bone with bone, cartilage,
ligaments, membranes, are fashioned out
of the same primordial tissue,
and come into being pari passu with
the bones themselves.
The entire fabric has its soft parts and its hard,
its rigid and its flexible parts;
but until we disrupt and dismember its bony,
gristly, and fibrous parts one from another,
it exists simply as a "skeleton,"
as one integral and individual whole.

D'Arcy Thompson, ***On Growth and Form***

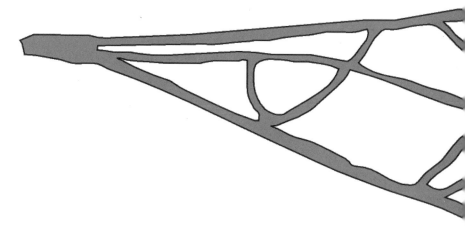

Clockwise from top. In its irregularity, the natural truss structure of D'Arcy Thompson's illustration of a
metacarpal bone from a vulture's wing prefigures the irregular, constructed tumbleweed truss.
A sea of irregular plaster swirls, designed by Jujol, sculpt the irregular
interiors and ceilings of Gaudí's Casa Milà.
Louis Sullivan began with the seed in developing and evolving his system of
ornamentation; perhaps the most successful translation of poetry,
botanics, and form in American architecture as seen in
the spandrel from his New York Bayard Building. 1897.
Foot Bridge, Ripol, Spain. 1992.
Santiago Calatrava, engineer.
Pergola, Can Negre. 1915. Sant Joan Despí, Barcelona.
Josep Maria Jujol, architect.

Exodesic

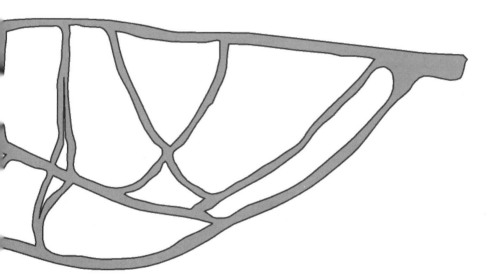

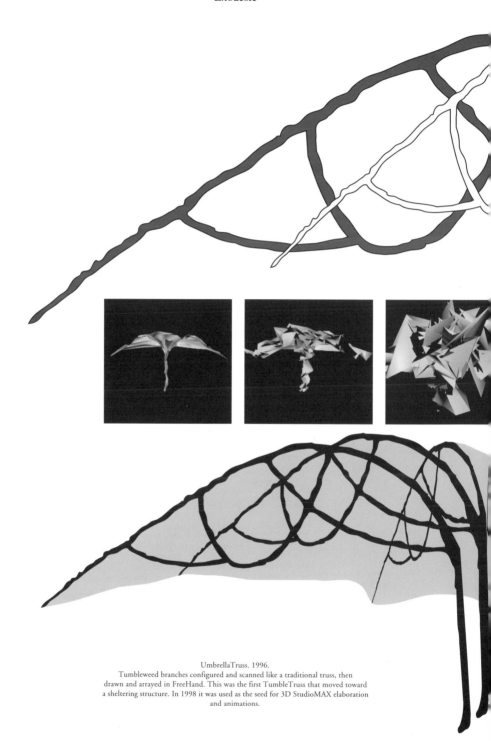

UmbrellaTruss. 1996.
Tumbleweed branches configured and scanned like a traditional truss, then
drawn and arrayed in FreeHand. This was the first TumbleTruss that moved toward
a sheltering structure. In 1998 it was used as the seed for 3D StudioMAX elaboration
and animations.

Exodesic

UmbrellaTruss II. 1998.
3D StudioMAX cells (bottom and right).
AutoCAD elevation (above).

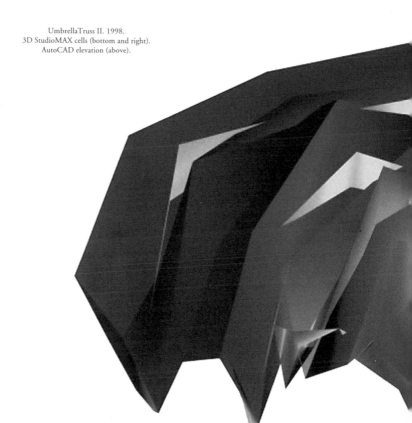

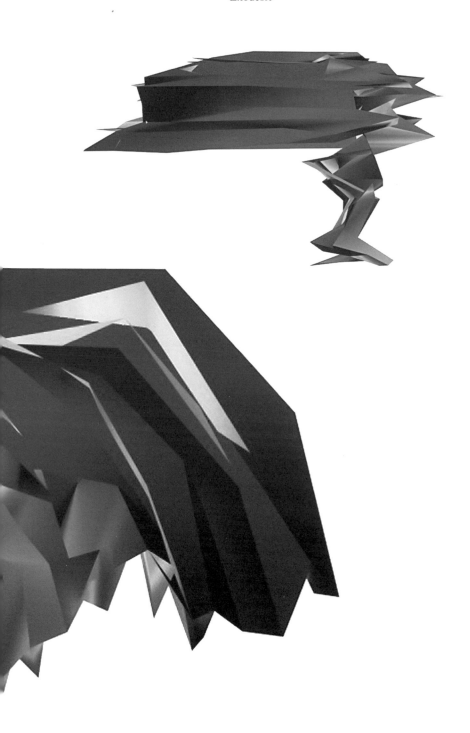

SampleTruss. 1996. 10" x 20" x 14".
Tumbleweed, copper wire, gauze, aluminum leaf, red thread, cedar (base).
One of several trusses used to test surface materials and methods.

Exodesic

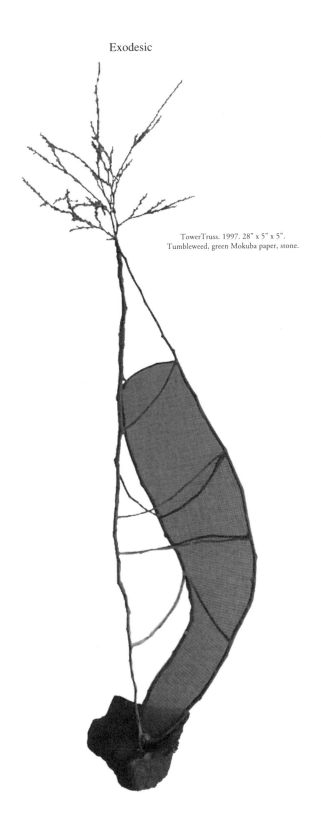

TowerTruss. 1997. 28" x 5" x 5".
Tumbleweed, green Mokuba paper, stone.

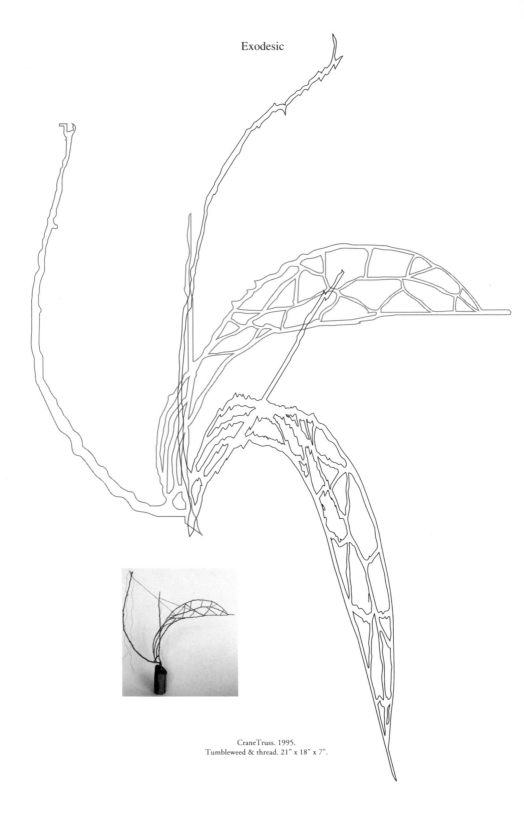

CraneTruss. 1995.
Tumbleweed & thread. 21" x 18" x 7".

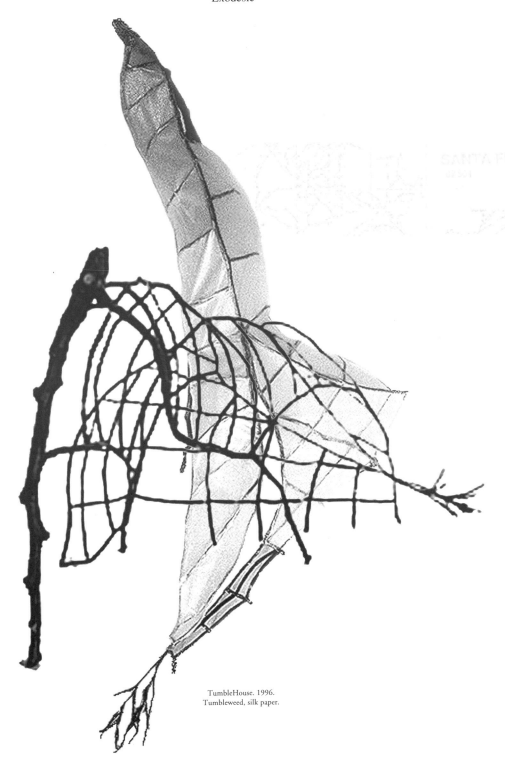

TumbleHouse. 1996.
Tumbleweed, silk paper.

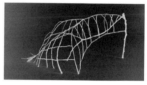

TumbleHouse. 1996. 8" x 24" x 27".
Tumbleweed, silk paper, gold leaf, corrugated cardboard.
(The corrugated structure is a studio/bedroom homage to New
Mexico's surviving Quonset huts.)

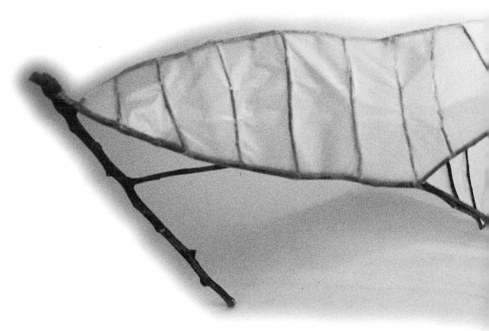

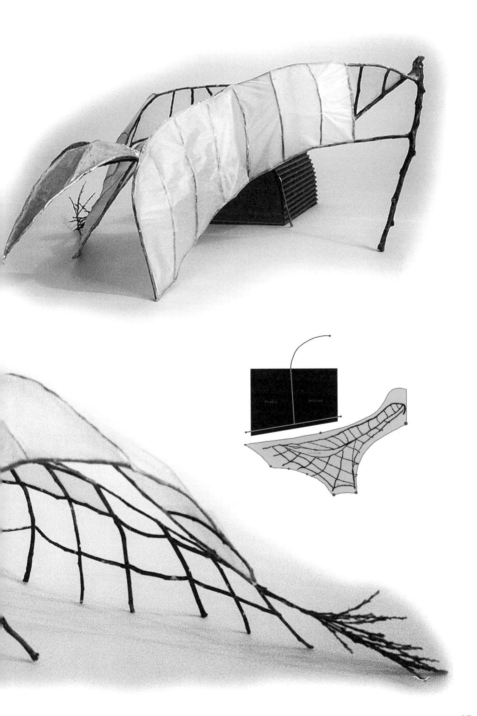

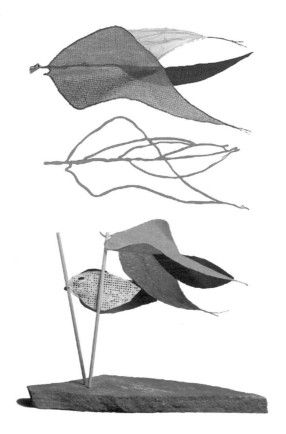

60sTruss. 1997. 10" x 10" x 8".
Tumbleweed, silver leaf, Mokuba paper, aluminum.
Drawing, tumbleweed frame (middle).

Cellular Structure

I've found only one source for more than cursory information regarding the morphology of tumbleweeds: the Web site Fire Effects Information System (FEIS) developed by the USDA Forest Service Intermountain Research Station's Fire Sciences Laboratory (IFSL) in Missoula, Montana (http://www.fs.fed.us/database/feis/plants/Forb/SALKAL/).

I've been more successful in finding a view into the tumbleweed's cellular structure. My sister, Terri Mallow, made it possible for Clinical Pathology Labs to prepare four slides that allowed me to look at the cellular structure of the tumbleweeds. The slide preparation, done by Mary A. Mullinax, H.T. (A.S.C.P.), was itself fascinating. Mary took a segment of a green tumbleweed, placed it in a tiny plastic cassette, and ran it through a vacuum infiltrating processor to halt degeneration of the cell structure, to dehydrate it, and then embed it in paraffin. With the paraffin holding the specimen she then sliced it on a microtome in 4-micron sections—this process is known as sectioning. The specimen is then bathed to remove wrinkles and picked up on a glass slide, drained, and placed on a warm plate to melt the paraffin and adhere the tissue to the glass. The slide is then bathed in a 13-step series of agents to stain the cell, and then it's cover-slipped. The specimens now offered the possibility of studying the cellular structure of the plant, and I began to contemplate using images of them in relation to the built models and the grown plants, as well as to place cellular images in the series of prints I make for each model. This segment of the project is ongoing, and I'm searching through this view of the plant's cells for ideas that can be related, even metaphorically, to the development of electronic growth or artificial life that, in turn, could generate autonomous structures—sort of cellular generator influencing the design path.

Viewing the tumbleweed slides without a microscope is futile, so I owe the sight of the beautiful cell structures to pathologist Dr. Pierr Johnson, who quickly agreed to show me the slides through his microscope at St Vincent Hospital in Santa Fe. We saw the slides magnified 40x, 100x, 400x. Later, Dr. Johnson photographed them at the magnifications we had viewed as well as at 1000x. It's from his photographs that I have begun to draw a developmental picture of the TumbleTruss Project that now moves from micro to macro and from analog to electronic. From cellular plant development through harvesting, from drying and building to virtual models, the project traces a view of live matter, inert forms, and virtual and analog structures.

Exodesic

Rear Elevation

Front Elevation

Left Elevation

NinjaTruss. 1997. 10" x 12" x 18".
Tumbleweed, Mokuba paper, clear plastic, silver leaf.
Progression from left: tumbleweed section, tumbleweed cells at 400x,
tumbleweed cells at 100x, NinjaTruss, overhead drawing, and three Extreme 3D
models based on the NinjaTruss.

Ninja Cell Walls. Barcelona, January 1997.
I outlined five cells from the 400x view of the tumbleweed cells and then
manipulated that drawing in FreeHand and Extreme 3D, creating
undulating wall forms and, later, web animations.

Forms emerge from forms, and others arise or descend from these. All are related, interwoven, intermeshed, interconnected, interblended. They exosmose and endosmose.
They sway and swirl and mix and drift interminably. They shape, they reform, they dissipate.
Louis H. Sullivan, *Kindergarten Chats*

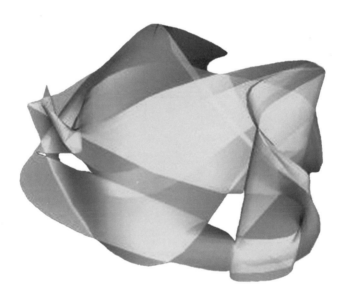

Warped exterior forms of the physical NinjaTruss model
transformed to generate interior space (above).
Extreme 3D NinjaTruss models (right).

It's over four years since I began the introductory text. Still, it remains the basic outline of the TumbleTruss Project. In the time since I last updated it, many small, but important developments have taken place. The most important is a working realization of the enormous difference between models, structures, and sculpture, and between big and small scale, when one is considering architecture or architectural sculpture. In terms of built work, the greatest development is in size. The first models vary from a few inches to approximately 24 inches; new works begin at about 36 inches and are currently reaching approximately 8 feet (and I intend for them to get bigger).

From the earliest models, paper and fabric were an integral part of my plans for the project. But the idea and push specifically to make paper came from Ronald Christ. It was Christ who prompted our mutual friend, Catalina Parra, to demonstrate papermaking for me. And during a week-long stay by Parra in Santa Fe, we made pulp and then paper. At this point I realized that possibilities existed not only to use the tumbleweeds from our site, but also to make pulp from almost anything growing around us. Later, I joined Christ (in our kitchen), while he laminated newly made paper sheets for his own project and I overlaid wet, newly made paper directly onto a TumbleTruss form. Then, as the sheathing and structural potential of making paper and directly covering the trusses became tangible, it became clear that I would need papermaking expertise. Here again Christ stepped in, facilitating an introduction to the papermaker with whom he was studying—Emily Watts, a Santa Fe-based artist and papermaker.

The first batch of pulp Watts made for the trusses was flax. She and I applied wet sheets to various forms, and we watched them dry in the hot sun behind her studio. To our surprise the paper totally deformed the trusses: its strength in drying—the shrinkage—pulled glued joints apart and totally rearranged the shape of the truss. This was thrilling—an unpredictable, random force adding change to the built trusses. Not only did I have readymade, complex-curved tumbleweed struts, but the skinning was also adding a semi-autonomous process of form distortion and unpredictability to the building process. After the first models, we experimented with thinner and more translucent (and hence weaker) sheets and learned to more carefully control drying and the skinning process. By this stage some of my bigger trusses were in the works, and we started to test, using wet sheets of paper, selectively inserted in a process resembling triangulation, to create stronger structural cells—adding strength in both tension and compression. My thought at the time was this: if the tumbleweed constructions could be made to support themselves based on a truss or cantilever, then structural paper could be included in the building process to induce greater strength, with the outcome of producing relatively big (over eight foot) spans from which some large-scale experimental structures could be produced. They, in turn, could be skinned with larger, connected sheets of paper.

During my first months working with Watts, she made various types of paper using flax and kenaf; she made them in various weights and dried them under differing conditions so that some sheets could be used for later ink-jet printing while others could be wetted and used in model building. In August I brought her two large Hefty bags full of thin-leaf yucca from our site. After a labor-intensive effort of removing the spikes, hammering and soaking the stalks, stripping off the flesh to get at the fiber, and then beating the fiber, she produced a pulp that yielded an off-white paper that when dried on a truss frame resembled skin. We used the yucca paper on both the BeamTruss and, more dramatically, on the truss that the flax had earlier distorted. I built a new inner structure that we covered with yucca, and this sort of dystopic, winglike model became known as the YuccaTruss (p. 44).

During the late summer of 1996, Watts also produced 8 sheets of thin flax paper, pressed and finished, which I began experimenting with to make some sort of curtain, screen, or flexible wall panels. I had two images in mind: soji screens and building shingles that I thought could be combined to produce something extralight that could be suspended from one of the large trusses. I wanted to use grommets to link sheets together, but I wanted that linkage to have something of the look of overlapping shingles. The first two sheets I connected with small grommets. I also punched two larger grommets in each sheet and then wedged through the grommet hole a branch of tumbleweed that acted as a stiffener while at the same time giving the paper shingle a curved form.

Exodesic

NoriTruss. 1997. 4" x 23" x 12".
Physical model: tumbleweed, Japanese paper, and handmade seaweed paper.
POV-Ray frame by Zeke Ricci (middle and upper right).
Extreme 3D model based on NoriTruss.

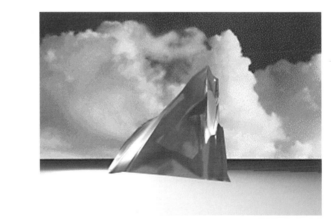

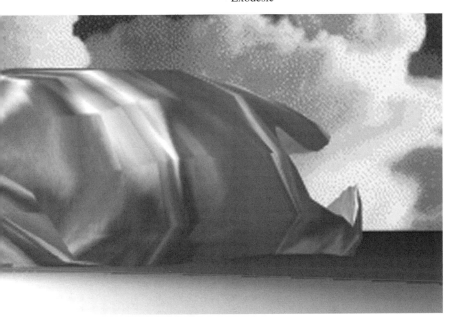

NoriTruss II. 1998. Side elevation (top). Extreme 3D models.
Front (left) and back (right) elevations.
Top (bottom left).

I'm not at all trying to pass the models (real or virtual) as architecture—yet. They are aspects of manipulated forms that could lead to the generation of architectural elements or segments; that said, I'm convinced that the conceptual process of searching for complex curves in nature or everyday items takes on an architectural relevance that is tectonic and mostly lost in architectural practice and education. The idea of finding some process that offers possibilities of form generation is one path in a search for architectural complexity. Where the forms generated by building models with tumbleweed struts is mostly arbitrary and dictated by my education and exposure, it's a process that is to a large degree mostly removed from current architectural fashion. And while the forms may look something like sets for *Mad Max: Beyond the Thunderdome,* they don't look theoretically driven. I want to think of them as forms manipulated from a nonrepetitive kit of abstract pieces that can be physically and digitally manipulated to present undulating forms appropriate to, and pleasing for, enhanced fluidity in enclosing and sculpting space.

Several projects turn out to have important influences for me and the TumbleTruss Project. In the wide spectrum is Duncan Brown's DuneRay/ ZenLux. To oversimplify: Brown experimented with Juan Gris's 1913 painting *Breakfast,* extrapolating from its computerized image a series of folds, rotations, and extensions until he had created a series of digital constructions (sometimes visually unrelated to *Breakfast*) that evolved into a framework for considering and constructing architectural models, projects, and interiors. This project has stayed in my view as an overall approach, even a system, for dealing with new and old technology, design, and architecture. And, in all its evolving guises, it's beautiful.

During a visit to Studio Associates, model builders in New York, I saw a laser-cut truss by Reiser + Umemoto. I was never able to put the truss out of my mind for very long, and it directly made me consider trusses as a typology in and of themselves. Now that I've seen the building it was designed for, the Yokohama Port Terminal, I'm reminded that amorphous structures, supported with engineering, are open areas for investigation.

I've known and greatly admired the work of Enric Miralles since before publishing and curating his first American book and exhibition. In discussions and in published interviews I've followed his statements as well as his work—I especially like his notion (echoing William Carlos Williams) that "ideas are in things." But it's his Huesca Sports Arena, especially its tripartite columns, that is etched in my mind's eye, that affects TumbleTrusses. The simple canting of three columns creating one of the most dancelike postures and painterly stances in architecture continually reminds me that objects and materials never need be what they seem or, in fact, really are. Here is an example of ideas embodied in things. Not only is the form appealing to me, it sets me looking for ideas for my own work.

3D StudioMAX

From the first, electronics has been part of the TumbleTruss Project. I began manipulating images in Photoshop and FreeHand simultaneously with physical model building. Mostly this entailed either scanning images or directly transferring digital photographs, adjusting color and contrast, filtering, silhouetting, retouching, etc. I've also drawn, rendered, and animated Extreme 3D and MAX models and have taken screen shots and then incorporated the images into the print graphics. I'm working toward a series of electronic models and animations, loosely based on the built TumbleTrusses, which can be experimented with to produce further multiple-curved forms in the semblance of surfaces or structures. Such models will extend the forms derived from the analog models into a series of form-typologies that may then be sampled and recomposed, creating a shape grammar of potential warped surfaces, which, in turn, could be applied to building surfaces. Furthermore, the electronic components plug seamlessly (sometimes) into CyberStudio for Web presentation in a native, digital environment. With the Web there is a flexible, somewhat dynamic theatrical site where animations and VRML worlds present aspects of the trusses that would otherwise be limited to gallery settings, print media, or video.

Because this project is always hovering in the betweens of analog and digital, architecture and sculpture, 2D and 3D, I realized that more powerful electronic forms were going to be necessary to communicate the TumbleTruss structures as well as to create environments for them to survive in. As the potential for larger-scale works grows, so does the need to communicate their structure through drawings. And, as the digital models progress and deviate from the tumbleweed and paper models, the need to reestablish them physically—most likely through stereolithography—starts to become a concern. 3D StudioMAX then becomes my primary focus for digital modeling with AutoCAD playing a support role for sections and elevations.

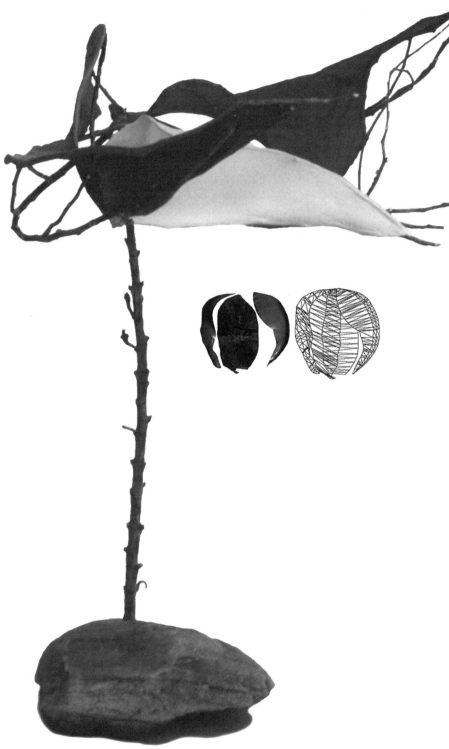

YuccaTruss. 1997. 20" x 17" x 18".
Tumbleweed, yucca stalk, stone, handmade yucca and flax papers.
Wireframe and rendering, Extreme 3D.

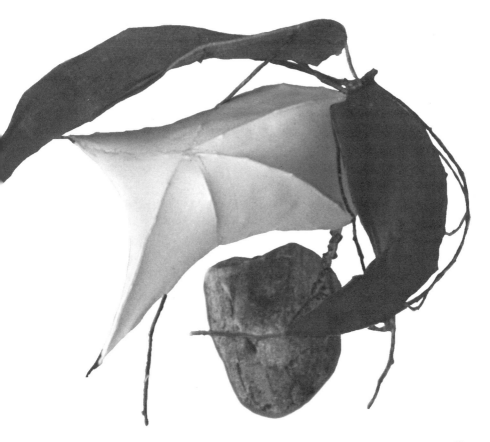

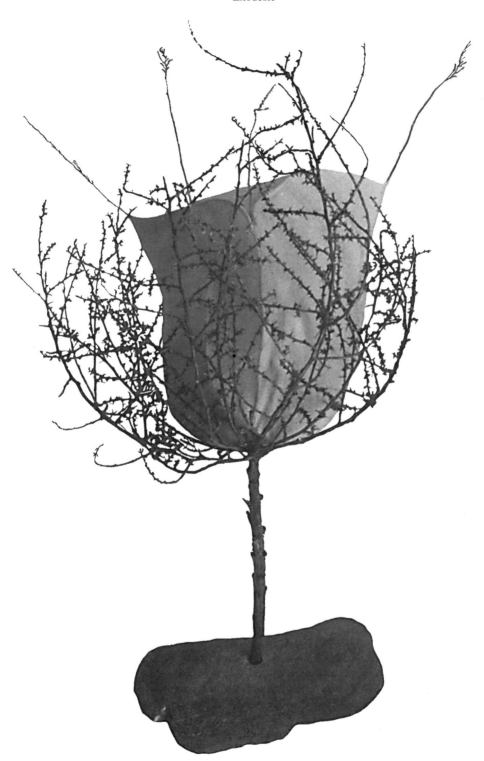

Exodesic

WeedTruss. 1997. 25" x 23" x 18".
Tumbleweed, yucca stalk, stone, handmade yucca paper.
My intention in this model was not only to create a canopy
but also to insert it within a section of the spherical, untrimmed weed.

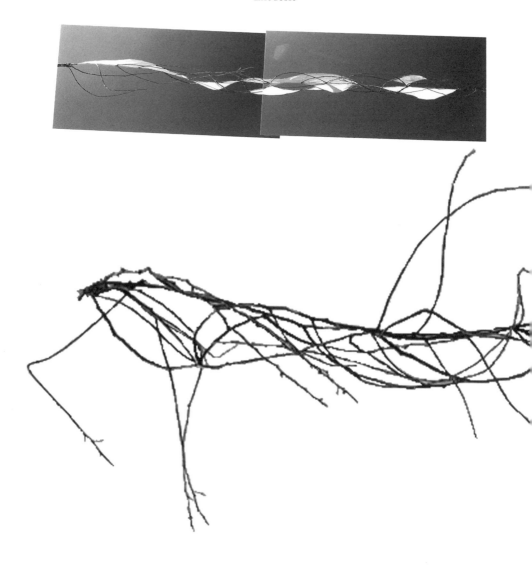

BeamTruss (top). 1997. 17' x 10" x 18".
Tumbleweed, handmade flax and yucca paper.
BigTruss. 1997. 5' x 15" x 15". Tumbleweed.
Truss with Red Paper Joints (right). 1997. 5' x 24" x 12".
Tumbleweed and Thai banana paper.
These structures were experiments in extending the truss
metaphor to mulitple-curved branches in order to build irregularly
triangulated, anchored, and cantilevered models.

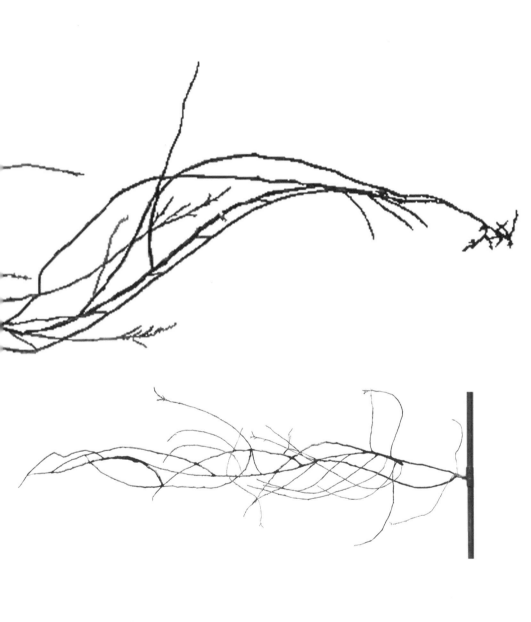

Exodesic

CantileverTruss. 1997. 5'8" x 3' x 15".
Tumbleweed, yucca stalk, Thai banana paper (on joints), handmade yucca paper.

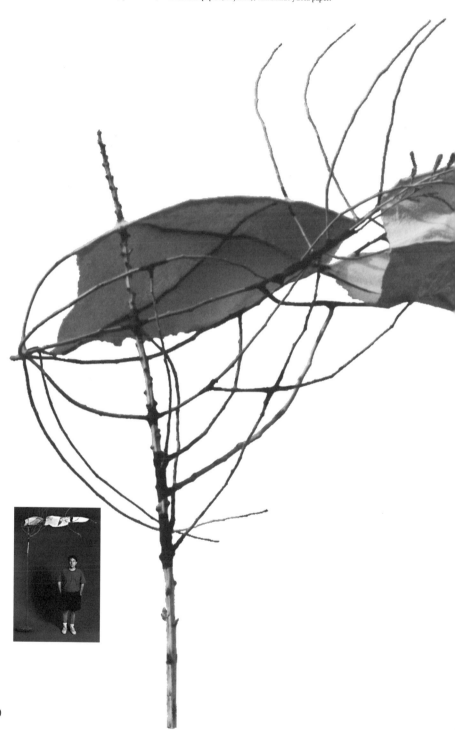

SamuraiTruss. 1997. 6'6" x 4' x 3'.
Tumbleweed, handmade cotton paper, gauze, copper pipe, stone.

Plan B. November 2, 1997

Met with Zane Fischer at Plan B and got a key to the gallery. Our discussions began in 1996 when I introduced myself and work to him at the experimental space called OffSite he was codirecting with Michael Lujan. After our initial discussions I began to concentrate on larger truss segments that later appeared at Plan B and that I intend to develop further into larger wall and ceiling segments and, maybe, full enclosures. In an unexpected development Zane and Michael closed OffSite and took over The Center for Contemporary Arts—changing its name to Plan B. Thus, the gallery that TumbleTruss Project was mounted in is a former National Guard tank repair garage. It's very big—exhibition space taking only about half of the overall area with an approximate 50 x 60-foot area. A beautiful space, with an arched wood roof supported on steel trusses—an excellent and subtle housing for my weak, abstract, and structurally subversive tumbleweed structures.

Over the spring and summer I intensified work, had photographs taken, sent out press releases, and tried to organize so that I could begin installing the show without having to fabricate things in the gallery. In addition, I also intensified graphic and Web work and searched for some sort of means of a quick-and-dirty system for exhibiting plotter and laserjet prints.

Tuesday/Wednesday. November 3 & 4. Began trucking the bigger pieces to the gallery while Ronald brought his car full of stuff. He begins photographing the installation process while I drill and mount pipe fittings to support the bamboo and copper poles. The floor has a concrete module, 4 x 6 feet with 3-inch wood frames gridding the slabs. I drill the wood areas while also paying attention to the remnants of the tank parking bays painted in black and white checked lines. These worn trace-lines counter the orthogonal wood grid and suggest a sort of angular orientation for sight lines through the trusses to the Web monitor.

I tried sewing laserjet prints onto spinnaker cloth and grommeting holes in the cloth for hanging. I test-mounted a few of these spinnaker graphics off of a cable 5 inches out from the wall so that when the gallery leaks, the water runs down the wall and misses the prints and phtotgraphs. They look sort of like graphic-clothes on a line. Continued mounting canopies on the bamboo poles and trusses on copper poles—they range in height from 7 to 12.5 feet.

Friday/Wednesday. November 6-12. Still mounting canopies and trusses. Situate glass and wood stands for the smaller models. Mount large ge-

Exodesic

Mockup for Plan B's Canopy Grove. 1997.
Tumbleweed frames covered with handmade yucca paper and mounted on bamboo poles.
Extreme 3D study for Canopy Grove (bottom).
Roxy and me during driveway assembly/scale test.

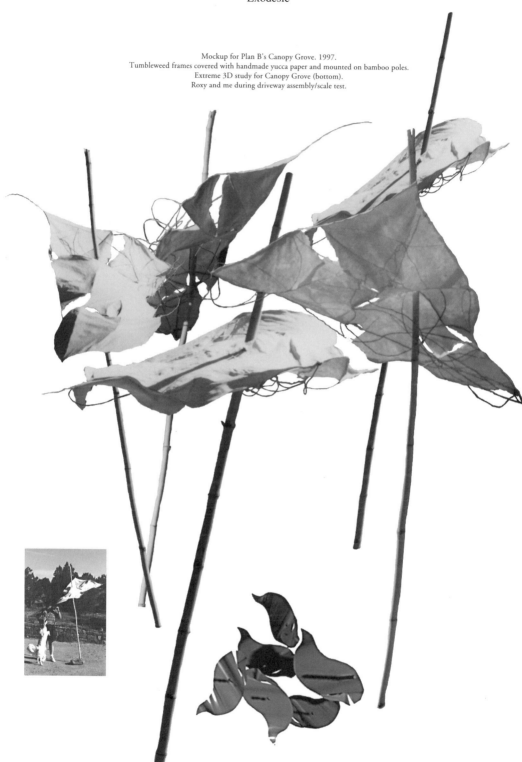

clay prints and NovaJet plotter prints. Install Web kiosk with modified Web site to serve as a catalog.

The bottom of Plan B's steel trusses are 16 feet above the floor (the ceiling is another 2.5 or 3 feet above that). I built two 8-foot-long mounts that clamp to the trusses and suspend a 7-foot TumbleTruss under its real cousin.

On Friday Woody and Steina Vasulka came by with a small video projector, tape deck, and sample tape, and we experimented with projections on the largest screen—testing its projection from the floor, from 8 to 10 feet above the floor, from eye level, and from the corners of the room. The resulting projections are encouraging, sometimes beautiful, and we decided to continue working together as a preliminary to future collaboration.

Steina agrees to meet Saturday night to further explore images and the structure's response to them, as well as how screen/ structures could be developed in future works. She leaves me with three tapes to select images from—I am most interested in the images of fire she made in a tape collaboration with Tom Joyce but also select a minute or two of water and steam images that sometimes suggest enlarged views of growing cellular life. Steina later edits a loop of the images for use at the opening.

Thursday. November 13. I see the current *Santa Fe Reporter,* and it has a photograph and notice for the show. Meet at Plan B with photographer and shoot the exhibition. Michael does lighting so that the gallery walls have a wash of brightness while the central canopies and trusses are lit on a reostat so that we can dim the big pieces to see the video.

Friday. November 14. *Pasatiempo* is published and includes an article on me and the work. Very flattering and well written with a photograph. Snow begins to fall around 11 a.m. and continues all day. Meet at 3:30 with videographer to document the show. Freezing. Zane brings in two butane heaters—they help, but it's still very cold, and it becomes apparent that many folks will not be able to drive to the opening. My guess is that around 100 people stop by.

Photo insert: warped surface of one of the canopies with fire projected video.

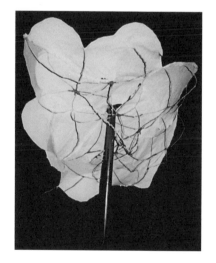

TumbleTruss Project
at Plan B, Santa Fe.
November-December 1997.
Installation shots (above left and right).
Details: Canopies' underside (left) and top (right).

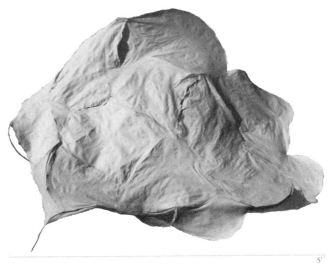

5'

West wall, Plan B
Sewn graphics on spinnaker cloth suspended on a stressed cable.
Spinnaker-graphic of the TumbleHouse (right). 12" x 15".

Graphic Screens

In March 1996, on a trip to New York, I took SyQuest files of the TumbleHouse and had an Iris print made. This 16 x 20-inch print was an experiment to test bigger prints than I can make with my equipment and to push a bit further in creating reproductions. After framing and studying it, I decided to move on with a series of prints. But, since the output of electronic graphics results in an analog object, I decided to distinguish the Iris prints from the related Web graphics by incorporating other elements onto the finished print. So, with later prints I began grommeting tissue overlays and photographs. Sort of collages.

By October '97 I had abandoned Iris prints and was experimenting with NovaJet plotter images on a much larger scale—up to 48 x 60 inches. I wanted the images to carry more information than what was on the printed plane so I continued attaching fragments of other prints and materials. Although they were coming closer to art objects, I still wanted them to convey layers of information even if bits of that collaged info disturbed or interrupted the primary image.

For the Plan B exhibition I needed to include graphics, but I decided they should seem temporary, transitional, and cheap, not a variation of framed gallery standards. After frustrating results from attaching test prints to glass and acetate, I tried sewing them onto spinnaker cloth—that thin, crisp, technical nylon used for spinnaker sails on racing boats. I got my mother to give me an old sewing machine and my sister to teach me how to wind bobbins, and I went for the zig-zag. By overlapping and sewing inkjet prints (or parts of them) with photos, I made a series of 23 spinnaker scrolls that I hung on a suspended and weighted, 30-foot cable—a floppy, clothesline of fabric and graphics.

Happy with the result of sewing images on spinnaker, I tried sewing onto irregularly sized pieces of screen mesh and then grommeting several sheets into a unit of overlays. This not only created physical layers, the semitransparency of the mesh made it obvious that to see the lurking, backgrounded images one could merely lift the screen veils. This veiling and leafing system, in turn, obscures the images, drawings, and sometimes text, making a series of layers that readers may move through. It literally and figuratively gives the graphics a backup file that begins to suggest a connection to other parts of the overall project—information of a primary and secondary nature. I also like the moiré patterns the sandwiched screens produce.

Screen I. 1997. 16" x 17".
Window screen, grommets, metalic thread, inkjet, laser, and photographic prints.

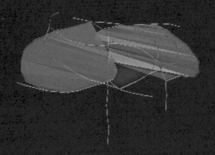

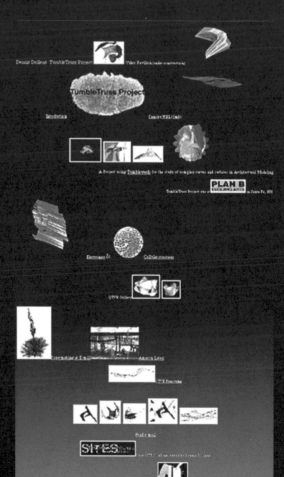

Cosmoplayer with SpiralTruss VRML (top).
The fully scrolled (www.rt66.com/~sites) TumbleTruss Project home page (bottom).

Exodesic

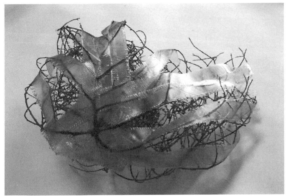

ToxicTruss. 1998. 9" x11" x 20".
This was an attempt to produce a skin that would conform to and envelope an entire tumbleweed. It turned out to be a misguided venture on my part because of the toxic nature of resin and woven glass. Still the results are interesting for creating a hard, structural skin and for the technical beauty of the semitransparency. Clearly this one gets an "F" grade in the environmental materials category. (Please e-mail me with suggestions for a more appropriate material with similar resulting qualities.)

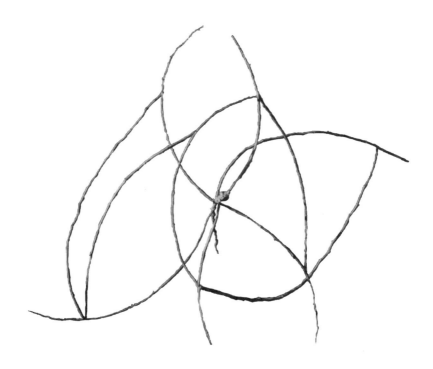

SpiralTruss. 1998. 12" x 22" x 15".
Tumbleweed frame (above).
Tumbleweed and Mokuba paper (right).
3D StudioMAX frames (below).

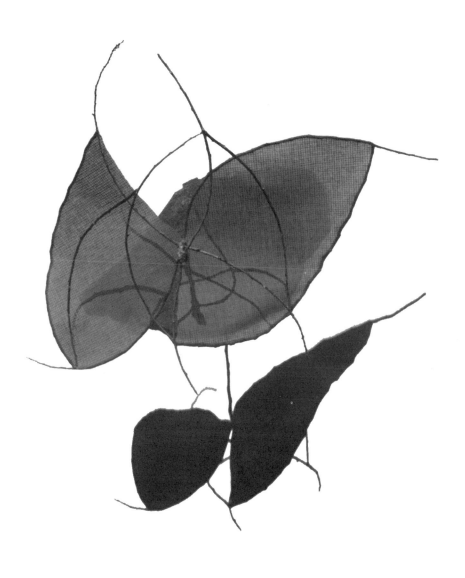

Exodesic

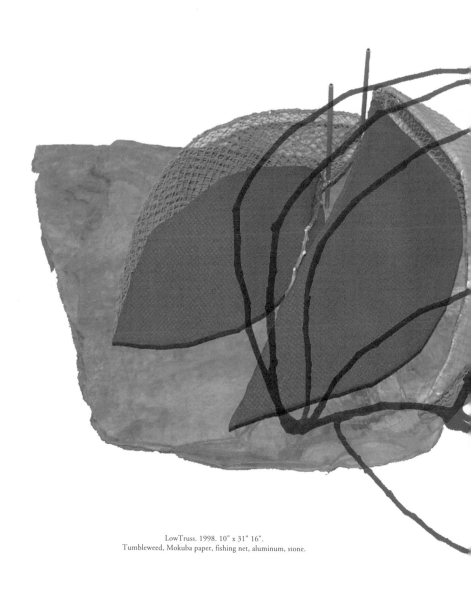

LowTruss. 1998. 10" x 31" 16".
Tumbleweed, Mokuba paper, fishing net, aluminum, stone.

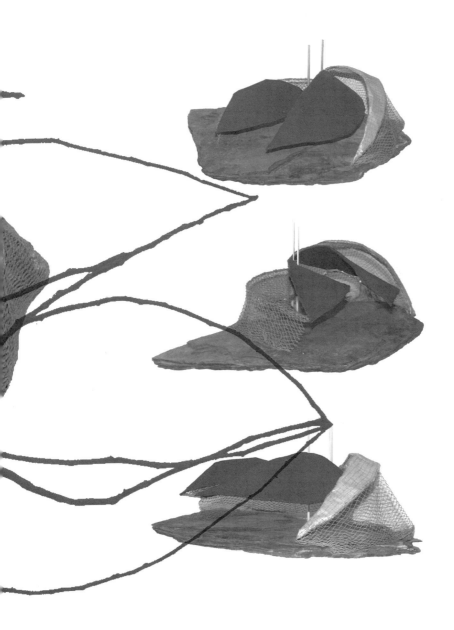

Amazon Latex

November 22, 1997. Leave for Brasilia. After 24 hours of travel and delays, we are met at the Brasilia airport by Valeria Cabral from the Athos Bulcão Foundation (our cohost along with the University of Brasilia) and taken to the Kubitschek Plaza Hotel.

November 24. Began seeing Niemeyer projects with Bulcão's collaborative works—mostly ceramic walls, dividers, and facades—and later had supper with Bia Medeiros from the university's faculty of art. We discuss plans for our lectures, and it was decided that I would present electronic architecture the next day with Ronald following on Wednesday with his presentation of the Vasulka's video and installation art, and with our joint presentation of our Jujol/Gaudí and Barcelona Pavilion tapes on Thursday.

During supper we met Maria Luiza Fragaso (Malu), an artist and professor of art at the university, and the surprise of the trip began to unfold as she discussed the work of Floriano Pastore, a professor of chemistry who is researching the potential of new materials from the  Amazon. Specifically, we were told about his developing chemical agents that aid in the production, formation, and preservation of latex at the same time that he is trying to organize, fund, and make commercially viable small-scale production of latex by families in the Amazon region. Malu's connection with

him is based on a theatrical collaboration, where the latex will be used for the production of sets.

Because I've been searching for materials to use in larger truss walls and because of the environmental connections already established with yucca papermaking and tumbleweed armatures in the TumbleTruss Project, Pastore's venture seemed a good opportunity to expand the project's scope of structural and environmental material while also establishing another collaborative link. After describing her collaborative plans with Professor Pastore, I asked if Malu would introduce us to him, which she did two days later.

Arriving at the chemistry department, we were first met by a graduate student and saw her applications of latex to sculptural forms of the human body. We also examined the raw liquid latex and the coagulant used to solidify it. We were shown samples of various latex sheets from the Amazon: sheets varying in thickness and surface patterns as well as sheets varying in color, anywhere from cream to amber to red, depending on the natural additives. We played with and stretched the sample sheets, and Professor Pastore described his efforts to establish this type of rubber production as an Amazonian cottage industry that might

supply economically desperate families with a means of income—an impressive goal under any circumstances, but one that grew more impressive when he cited his research statistics analyzing the ratio of latex production to the burning of the jungle. His statistics show that a direct correlation exists:

burning of the jungle is inversely proportionate to increased rubber-latex production—sort of a win-win proposition—except that no real market yet exists for the latex sheets.

The method of producing the latex sheets requires tapping and collecting raw rubber liquid, mixing it with a coagulant, and pouring it into small trays where it coagulates into sheets after about ninety minutes. The wet sheets are then fed through a hand press, something like the rollers of old-fashioned washing machines, rolled into thinner sheets, and finally hung on lines to dry in the roofed but open-sided drying sheds.

Photographs, page 68:
Materials arriving at Gurupa (top); Training in the Amazon, Professor Pastore second from the right.
Page 69:
Tapper in his working shed (top); Rubber hung to dry (middle); Tapper with a latex sheet.

I showed Pastore photographs of my exhibit at Plan B and described the analog and digital models, structures, and graphics, as well as ideas for further development that may include the use of video projection. We discussed the possibility of custom production of 500 latex sheets for use in an experimental structure that I would develop and build in New Mexico. These sheets will be 1 mm thick and light cream colored to achieve as much translucency as possible in order for the video projection to be visible on both sides. Since I'm interested in larger sheets than are currently produced, Pastore agreed to manufacture larger presses and formation vats. He also immediately decided to contact a family headed by two brothers for the work, knowing their facilities and abilities to carry out this order.

This collaboration, we both understand, is of little economic importance; some value lies in the possibility of small-scale adaptations of current working methods, but its real potential lies in the possibility of public information centering on social and environmental issues that are at the foundation of Pastore's research and the implications of his project. Additionally, from my perspective, our working together points out possibilities for small-scale collaborations where handmade materials—in this case a kind of industrial craft—can be brought together with experimental forms that rely on artistic and electronic elaboration in order to complete a structural unit. In this sense, there is a hybrid creation, a crossover between analog construction and digital transformation that helps me to think about, draw, and build spatial volumes, irregular surfaces, and digital mutations initially derived from plant forms and materials.

Currently (fall 98), I'm working with sheets of latex Professor Pastore gave me. Using them involves a scaling up from previous models, and I'm working with cedar branches from our site to replace the tumbleweed truss struts. The structural upscaling is necessary to support the weight and elasticity of the latex sheets. And to support both the branch trusses and latex, I've cast three concrete columns outside our house. This mock up, provisionally called AmazonTruss, will be triangular, approximately 8' x 8' x 8' canted at 3' to 7' feet above the ground and will allow projectors to be placed both inside and out to evualate the structure as a screen roof/wall.

Simultaneously, I'm building a Max structure, thinking that the physical and virtual designs may come together in the form of a pavilion for video and Web projection.

Exodesic

Cast and sculpted columns for AmazonTruss (above).
3D Studio Max studies for AmazonTusss digital projection structure (below).

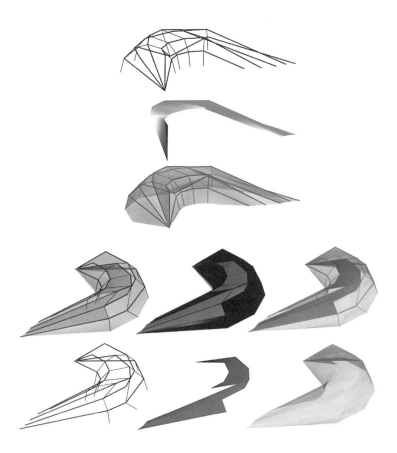

Exodesic

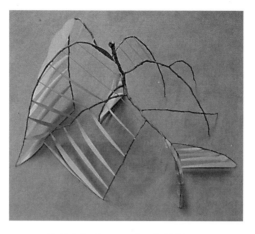

Model airplane forms reconfigured in FoilTruss.

Exodesic draws together three years of models, graphics, electronics, craft, and writing that fall
under my rubric of the TumbleTruss Project. Many of the works presented here
will tumble on in different forms in various media.
Surf **www.rt66.com/~sites** for further development.

Tumbleweeds as Movie Stars

The Sons of the Pioneers's recording of *Tumbling Tumbleweeds* not only rolls through
Ronald Christ's *ex*ODE (p 6), it also opens Joel and Ethan Coen's movie
The Big Lebowski. Along with that movie-star weed, tumbling, rolling, blowing through Los Angeles (like
the roll-ons its plant forbears made in many a Western movie) the name reminds us that
Tumbling Tumbleweeds is also the title of Gene Autry's 1935 film. Among other star vehicles for the barby
weed, an entire episode of *The Outer Limits* stands high in my kitsch-esteem; it features
Eddie Albert and June Havoc along with the ensemble acting of hundreds of fine weeds.
In this episode, called *Cry of Silence*, the sentient S. Kali trap and attempt to kill the 1964 production's
hero and heroine in a "living nightmare populated with killer tumbleweeds."
Cry of Silence should be remembered as a benchmark in the recognition of botanic intelligence.

Project Software:
Photoshop 4.0
FreeHand 7 & 8.0
Extreme 3D
3D StudioMAX r2
AutoCAD
WordPerfect 3.5
CyberStudio 3
CosmoPlayer

TumbleTruss
project